T0198897

IT'S GOING TO RAIN

THE STORY OF NOAH AND HIS FAMILY.

BY

MIRTHELL BAZEMORE

AuthorHouse™
1663 Liberty Drive
Bloomington, IN 47403
www.authorhouse.com
Phone: 1 (800) 839-8640

Because of the dynamic nature of the Internet, any web addresses or links contained in this book may have changed since publication and may no longer be valid. The views expressed in this work are solely those of the author and do not necessarily reflect the views of the publisher, and the publisher hereby disclaims any responsibility for them.

Any people depicted in stock imagery provided by Getty Images are models, and such images are being used for illustrative purposes only.
Certain stock imagery © Getty Images.

Interior Image Credit: JONASIA M. BLOUNT & NIQUASHA HICKSON

This book is printed on acid-free paper.

ISBN: 978-1-7283-5834-5 (sc)
978-1-7283-5833-8 (e)

Print information available on the last page.

Published by AuthorHouse 04/03/2020

authorHOUSE®

Edited
By
Sandra Gregg

Illustrations By
Jonasia Blount & Niquasha Hickson

"The Lord Equips His People to Work"

Thankful and Grateful,

   I was inspired to write "It's Going to Rain" because our young children need to be reminded of the historical event that took place during the time of Noah.

   The story of Noah's Ark teaches us how the Lord our God was troubled and disappointed with the disobedience and immoral behavior of mankind and the repercussions of such behavior ~ Destruction.

   In July 2019 I had the opportunity to visit the Ark Encounter located in Williamstown, Kentucky by recommendation of my Publishing Agent Buddy Dow of AuthorHouse. Though it is not the actual Ark, the replicate itself had a profound effect on me, which was humility, and gratitude.

   I give honor and thanks to my Lord and Savior Jesus Christ for giving me the gift of writing, as I encourage others to write and share their God given gifts. I am thankful for my husband, mentor and friend Lionel Bazemore and my daughter Sandie Bazemore whom have supported my work for years.

   I am grateful to God for the Holy Scriptures he left us to bear record of his existence and direction; my Church family and Pastor Bishop Joe C Tisdale who continues to preach Gods truth to this untoward generation, and calling ALL men unto repentance before it's too late, as it is certain that we are now in the days of Noah.

   Finally those who had assisted me on this book project including my sister in Christ and Editor Sandra Gregg who has worked diligently with children in the South Carolina public school systems as an educator, while representing a woman of holiness.

   Special gratitude to Min and Sis Blount and Sis Latoya Rich for embracing their children's artistic gift as well as Min and Sis Smith for their support; Bro and Sis South and all those who kept me encouraged on my journey... Thank you.

Sis Mirthell Bazemore

The LORD then said to Noah,
"Go into the ark, you and your whole family, because
I have found you righteous in this generation.

LONG AGO, THERE LIVED A MAN NAMED NOAH. THE LORD FAVORED NOAH BECAUSE HE WAS FAITHFUL, OBEDIENT AND HE FEARED GOD.

NOAH AND HIS WIFE HAD THREE SONS.

HIS SONS NAMES WERE SHEM, JAPETH AND HAM WHO WERE ALL MARRIED.

DURING THE TIME OF NOAH, THE WORLD HAD CHANGED
AND THE PEOPLE BECAME WICKED.

THEY WERE DISOBEDIENT AND HAD NO FEAR OF GOD,
AND THEIR BEHAVIORS WERE IMMORAL.

THIS TROUBLED THE LORD...SO HE SPOKE TO NOAH.

THE LORD WAS SO TROUBLED BY THE BEHAVIOR OF MANKIND...THAT HE DECIDED TO DESTROY THE INHABITANTS OF THE EARTH BY WATER.

THIS DESTRUCTION WOULD DESTROY EVERYTHING AND EVERYONE, EXCEPT NOAH, HIS FAMILY AND THE ANIMALS THAT WERE PAIRED TO GO ONTO THE ARK.

SURPRISINGLY, IT HAD NEVER RAINED BEFORE. BUT WHEN GOD SPOKE TO NOAH AND TOLD HIM "IT'S GOING TO RAIN" NOAH BELIEVED IT AND PREACHED IT TO WARN THE PEOPLE.

OF COURSE, THEY DID NOT LISTEN AND CONTINUED THEIR WICKED AND IMMORAL WAYS.

THE LORD GAVE NOAH THE DIMENSIONS OF THE ARK AND HE AND HIS SONS BEGAN WORKING VERY DILIGENTLY TO BUILD IT.

The length 300 Cubits

The breadth 50 Cubits

The height 30 Cubits

HE TOLD HIS SONS THAT GOD COMMANDED HIM TO BUILD THE ARK BECAUSE "IT'S GOING TO RAIN" AND NOW THEY MUST GATHER ALL THE ANIMALS, BOTH MALE AND FEMALE OF EACH KIND TO BRING INTO THE ARK.

IT TOOK NOAH ONE HUNDRED TWENTY YEARS TO BUILD THE ARK.

THERE WERE SO MANY ANIMALS TO BE GATHERED BY NOAH AND HIS SONS THAT THE LORD DID HELP.

THESE LIVING CREATURES WERE BLESSED BY GOD TO REPRESENT THEIR SPECIES.

ALL THE LIVING CREATURES WITH THEIR MATES WERE READYING TO GO INTO NOAH'S ARK, BECAUSE

"IT'S GOING TO RAIN"

WHILE NOAH WAS COMPLETING THE BUILDING OF THE ARK, THE WIVES WORKED HARD TOO.

THEY BROUGHT FOOD AND SUPPLIES AS NEEDED.

NOAH ALSO HAD HIS PLACE OF WORSHIP, AS HE LOVED HIS LORD THY GOD.

AS THE ARK WAS NEARLY COMPLETED, THE PEOPLE CONTINUED TO MOCK NOAH AND STILL DID NOT BELIEVE.

EVENTHOUGH, ALL THE ANIMALS HEADED TOWARDS THE ARK IN PAIRS, THEY STILL DID NOT BELIEVE.

FINALLY, THE ARK WAS COMPLETED AND ALL THE ANIMALS WERE DISCRETELY PLACED IN THEIR LIVING QUARTERS, AS GOD'S WILL - WAS DONE.

THE FOUR WIVES THEN ENTERED INTO THE ARK.

THE SKIES BECAME OVERCAST AND DARKENED WITH BOLTS OF LIGHTENING...THE PEOPLE BECAME AFRAID, BUT IT WAS TOO LATE!

NOAH AND HIS SONS TRIED TO CLOSE THE DOOR TO THE ARK, BUT IT WAS TOO HEAVY.

HE WAS THEN COMMANDED BY GOD TO GO INSIDE THE ARK, WHILE THE LORD DID THE REST.

NOW THAT NOAH'S FAMILY OF EIGHT MEMBERS WERE SAFELY INSIDE THE ARK,

THE LORD GOD ALMIGHTY SHUT THE DOOR.

SUDDENLY...

THUNDER ROARED AND LIGHTNING LIT UP THE SKY.

THE PEOPLE OF THE EARTH OF ALL AGES, STARTED TO FEEL WATER DROP ONTO THEIR SKIN FROM THE SKY.

AT FIRST, A FEW DROPS FELL. THEN SUDDENLY, THERE WAS A DOWN POUR OF RAIN.

IT RAINED AS IF THE RAIN WOULD NEVER-EVER STOP.

THE WATER GREW AND GREW AND LIFTED UP THE ARK AND IT BEGAN TO MOVE.

THE PEOPLE OF ALL THE EARTH, BOTH YOUNG AND OLD BEGAN TO CRY FOR **HELP** AS THEY RAN TO TAKE SHELTER. AS GOD WOULD HAVE IT, THE WATER OVERPOWERED THEM AND THE EARTH WAS SOON COMPLETELY COVERED WITH WATER.

ALL LIVING THINGS ON THE EARTH WERE NOW DESTROYED, EXCEPT NOAH AND HIS FAMILY.

IT RAINED NONSTOP FOR FORTY DAYS AND FORTY NIGHTS.

THE EARTH WAS NOW ONE BIG OCEAN, AS THE SEA LIFE WAS ALSO SPARED.

AFTER FORTY DAYS AND NIGHTS THE RAIN STOPPED.

NOAH OPENED THE TOP WINDOW OF THE ARK AND SAW BLUE SKIES, BUT HE SAW NO EARTH IN SIGHT. SO, HE SENT OUT A RAVEN TO SEARCH FOR LAND.

THE RAVEN FLEW OUT BUT HAD NO PLACE TO REST, SO IT RETURNED BACK TO NOAH.

AFTER A FEW DAYS HAD PASSED, NOAH OPENED THE WINDOW AGAIN AND THIS TIME HE SENT OUT A DOVE.

THE DOVE RETURNED TO NOAH AFTER FLYING A SHORT DISTANCE WITH A FRESHLY PICKED OLIVE BRANCH, THAT HE GAVE TO NOAH.

WHEN NOAH LOOKED UP TOWARDS THE HEAVENS, HE WAS GRATEFUL TO GOD FOR SPARING HIS LIFE. HE SAW A BEAUTIFUL BRIGHT RAINBOW PLACED IN THE SKY AS A COVENANT FROM GOD TO NEVER AGAIN DESTROY THE EARTH BY WATER.

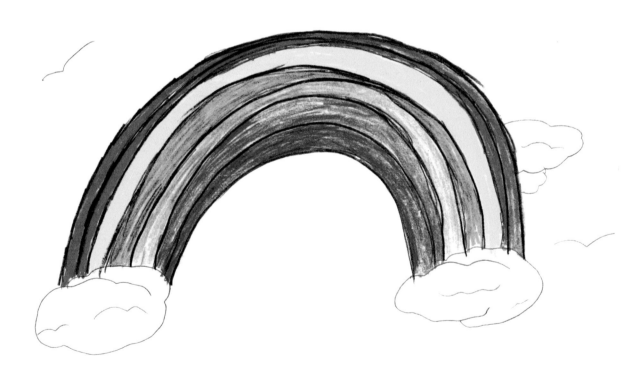

NOAH AND HIS FAMILY "PRAISED THE LORD" AS LAND WAS NEAR AND THEY COULD EXIT THE ARK AND RELEASE ALL OF GOD'S CREATURES BACK TO THE EARTH AND INTO THEIR NATURAL HABITATS.

THE LORD WAS PLEASED WITH NOAH FOR HIS FAITHFULNESS AND OBEDIENCE...WE ALL NEED TO BE OBEDIENT AND FAITHFUL LIKE NOAH - AND BE DEAR CHILDREN IN THE LORD.

"ONLY A FEW WERE SAVED"

THE END

ABOUT THE ILLUSTRATORS

Niquasha Hickson

Niquasha is a 17-year- old resident of Florence, S.C. During her sophomore and junior year she was an active member of ROTC/Air Force program, and held the rank of Airman First Class. She will be attending college to become an Anesthesiologist and also pursue a career in Computer Technology. Her hobbies are designing, drawing and expressing her creative energy through art.

"The few things I possess are things I would never want to lose. Whether it's a couple of grains of sand or a whole family full of support, I love and cherish them all."

Jonasia Blount

Jonasia is an 11-year-old resident of Portsmouth, VA. Her life's goal is to become an accomplished animator and to continue her love for the liberal arts. In her free time when she is not creating masterpieces, she enjoys the creative and imaginative works of Japanese culture. The support for her craft comes from a long list of family members, church family, and a close net of friends.

There's A Rainbow in the Sky

The Earth that God created was once beautiful land, but
the evilness of mankind, had to be put to an end.
God once found favor in a single man, we'll he find favor in us again?
A massive storm that last forty days and forty nights,
as evil was washed away in one single plight.
Noah built an ark and only eight were saved, while
the rest of mankind died in a watery grave.
After the Earth was washed clear, a rainbow was placed in the
sky; as a covenant from God that it will be fire the next time.
So remember, A rainbow is our constant
reminder, after rain has filled the sky
That our God, Lord and Savior...his time is at nigh.

By
Mirthell Bazemore

Printed in the United States
By Bookmasters